2008 HANCOCK LECTURE

THE WORLD IS
OUR BACKYARD

Individual Responsibility for a Global Society

Dr. Samantha Nutt

Published in 2008 by
The Hancock Lecture Committee
Hart House
University of Toronto
Toronto, Ontario, M5S 3H3
416-978-2452
www.harthouse.ca

Dr. Samantha Nutt
The World is Our Backyard:
Individual Responsibility for a Global Society

ISBN 978-0-9694382-8-1

Printed and Bound in Canada

FOREWORD

I am twenty-five years old and most of my life I have lived in an eerie penumbra between war and peace. I remember staying up late to watch the coverage of the first invasion of Iraq on TV with my parents. Then came Somalia, Rwanda, Yugoslavia, and finally Afghanistan and again Iraq, to name but a few. For much of this time, Canadian soldiers have been deployed in war zones. But what impact—aside from news dispatches and sometimes vigorous debate—has this state of war had on our daily lives? For many of us, very little.

Not so for Dr. Samantha Nutt, Founder and Executive Director of War Child Canada, who is delivering this year's Hancock Lecture on the themes of social justice, social responsibility in a global context, and the impacts of war. Dr. Nutt has spent over a decade doing humanitarian work in war zones and raising awareness about the impacts of violence back home, work for which she has been widely recognized. War Child Canada (www.warchild.ca) is operational in ten war-torn regions around the world, including Darfur, Afghanistan, Iraq, and the Democratic Republic of Congo, where it partners with local organizations to do innovative humanitarian work supporting women and children affected by war. Many musicians, including Radiohead and The Tragically Hip, have generously donated their talent to support War Child's awareness and fundraising efforts. In Canada, War Child offers a number of awareness and fundraising programs to encourage young people to get involved, including "Get Lou-d" and "Keep the Beat".

Indeed, Sam has found that youth—and their teachers—have been War Child's most energetic supporters. A provocative and engaging thinker, she fits neatly into the Hart House Lecture's tradition of sparking debate, reflection, and inquiry among young people on the pressing issues of the day. Launched in 2001 as an annual public lecture, the Hart House Lecture Series was supported until this year by Hart House's Warden, Margaret Hancock. From this year forward, as a tribute to her legacy in fostering student development, the annual Hart House Lecture has been renamed the Hancock Lecture.

Earlier this spring, I sat down with Dr. Nutt for a wide-ranging Q&A about her work, reproduced here as a complement to her lecture. We talked about the emotional consequences of working in war zones, the missing debate about Canada at war, the difficulties and rewards of getting people's attention, and War Child Canada's message and activities. Talking with Sam was like leaving the city, hiking up a tall mountain, breathing in the fresh air, and being overwhelmed by the view. So much of the public "debate" about war in this country sounds as if it's being read from the same script—whether it is a general, politician, academic expert, or media pundit delivering the talking points. In his classic 1946 essay "Politics in the English Language," George Orwell condemned the widespread use of euphemisms and "exhausted idioms" to defend the indefensible: "Defenseless villages are bombarded from the air, the inhabitants driven out into the countryside, the cattle machine-gunned, the huts set on fire with incendiary bullets: this is called pacification. Millions of peasants are robbed of their farms and sent trudging along the roads with no more than they can carry: this is called transfer of population or rectification of frontiers. People are imprisoned for years without trial, or shot in the back of the neck or sent to die of scurvy in Arctic lumber camps: this is called elimination of unreliable elements." How much has changed? We still read about collateral damage, staying the course, supporting the troops and—in a phrase Orwell mocked sixty years ago—standing shoulder to shoulder with whichever ally is politically expedient.

Sam has devoted her life to breaking through this fog, through her work on the ground and insistence on telling the human stories of war. In her lecture and the text that follows, she delivers frank reflections about the need for all of us to recognize our connection to conflicts around the world and to honestly reckon with the costs of war. Only then can we begin the journey toward living as socially responsible, global citizens.

Daniel Aldana Cohen
Toronto, March 2008

1

Introducing Dr. Samantha Nutt

How did you come to found War Child Canada?

I started War Child Canada in 1999 with two other people, Frank O'Dea, who helped found Second Cup as well as Street Kids International, and Dr. Steven Hick, a professor of Social Work at Carleton University. By this point in my life, I had already spent a considerable amount of time living and working in war torn countries, including Somalia (my first experience in a war zone at the age of 24), Liberia, Burundi, and Iraq. It became apparent to me, from these experiences, that there was a growing need for an organization dedicated specifically to the cause of war-affected children. In founding War Child Canada, we wanted build an organization that moved beyond traditional concepts of charity. We wanted to create something that would support and sustain excellence at the field level, working with local partners to meaningfully engage them in the process of rebuilding and rehabilitating their communities. We wanted to stay clear of setting up large administrative offices staffed with foreign personnel—it had to be grassroots and it had to be participatory at the local level. At the same time, we wanted to encourage public discourse around war, to bring global issues to the fore through education and awareness-building initiatives, as a means of fostering and promoting a more just, more sustainable, and more equitable world.

But the title of "founder" to me is something that many people deserve when it comes to War Child Canada. There are those of us who had our names on the first registration papers, but there are also those over the years who have brought their talent, their wisdom and their experience to the organization and have helped it grow and evolve. It's an organic process, and it's a title that many people are worthy of.

Why did you choose to work in the NGO (non-governmental organization) world instead of politics or government?

I think you can make a difference in a myriad of ways. Some people are better suited to the corridors of politics. But for me, the challenge of politics is the politics. To succeed in politics you have to be prepared to compromise. And at that point in my life, when I was starting War Child Canada, my field experiences made me very passionate about these issues; I was twenty-eight, and compromise was not part of my vocabulary. I was focused on effecting change through the most immediate, direct, and transparent means possible. For me that meant the NGO route as opposed to a larger organization, a multinational agency, or government.

I have read in a couple profiles that you are often so busy you do not have a lot of time to sleep. You have also spent a lot time with people who have suffered so much violence and despair. Were there moments when this made it hard to sleep?

There are many times when I've had a very hard time with all of it—never mind sleeping. I would be lying if I said I don't live with a lot of ghosts. I think that anybody who does this work feels the same way. You think about the people that you cared about that you've lost to war; the people you wanted to help and knew that you could help but were prevented from doing so because of circumstances within that country or circumstances within our own country where you just didn't have the resources. People I have been close to have paid with their lives as a result of the work they were doing and it can be really tough.

I have spent a lot of time in Iraq, starting in 1996. I was there in 2003 just after the fall of Saddam's statue and within eighteen months of that I had lost two close friends in very brutal, brutal ways. One, Aquila Al Hasheimi, was gunned down in front of her home. She was one of three women appointed to the interim governing council in Iraq. And the other was Margaret Hassan who was the head of CARE (an international relief and development organization) operations in Baghdad, and who had lived and worked in Iraq for thirty years. She was taken hostage on her way to the CARE office and eventually executed after she literally begged for her life in a video that aired on every major news channel for about a month. I remember, during that period of time—and it was just after we had lost Aquila—turning on the news and watching Margaret. I just felt sick. I was full of sadness and rage—how was this possible? Thousands of protestors in Iraq filled the streets demanding her release. A few months later she was dead.

With Margaret's death I was forced to confront the

inescapable reality that everything that I had always believed in—in terms of what it means to be a humanitarian, what it means to operate within a humanitarian space, that you are outside of the political process because you're helping, because your intentions are good—these rules no longer applied. I mean, Margaret was a brave woman doing the kind of work that I fervently believed in—engaging local communities with a high level of receptivity—and within Iraq she was a hero, she helped thousands and thousands of kids, she stayed during both aerial bombardments, she was married to an Iraqi, she was a dual Iraqi-British citizen, and if anyone should have been protected from that kind of violence, it should have been Margaret. And it didn't matter. She was targeted anyway. So everything that I believed up until that point in time about what it means to be a humanitarian died with Margaret. That was a really difficult period. There have been other really difficult times but that was one of the hardest.

We are in a new reality now and we have to be mindful of it. The lines between military and civilian humanitarian operations have become increasingly blurred in recent years. That changes the way aid workers are viewed on the ground, and it has profound implications for the humanitarian movement whether we want it to or not.

Does it get easier? Do you get used to these situations?

No. What you get used to is how to contextualize it. You get used to the transition between here and there, between your life here and your life there, between your work here and your work there. It's the ultimate paradox: You're here in your office in Toronto and on your computer, making plans for dinner and spending time with your husband and son, and then you are in the field and you are with people who have had their kids ripped from their arms—and in some cases thrown into fires, and tortured —their husbands shot in front of them, after the women were raped so that this would be their last living memory. And it is always horrible to know that this exists in the world— that never gets easier. For a long time, I found the transition back to my life here to be very frustrating. In my case, I eventually learned to appreciate everything I have instead of railing against it and being obnoxiously self-righteous (which I suspect I was for many of the early years).

You have clearly come across desperately difficult situations, where "solutions" are by necessity partial and provisional. How do you maintain a balance between critical realism and the optimism you need to do your work?

Well, as an organization we are actually pretty good about that. We spend a lot of time, particularly if we are launching a new program, participating in the evaluation process so that when we go into an area, we are reasonably confident that our programming is going to succeed. But you can never be confident about the risks. Even if a situation is okay for us to be programming in—Darfur is a perfect example—it changes on a dime, it is very, very volatile, and particularly when you have staff that are deployed, there are implications too. You have to constantly be on top of security, of other changing political and economic conditions, what impact these might have, and you have to modify your programming accordingly. Sometimes you scale up, sometimes you scale down. When we go in, we are in it for the long haul. When you work in war zones, you have to think about the long term. There is no context, at least not in a war zone, where it is bad for two months then everything is hunky-dory. It does not happen like that. If it is bad for two months then usually it is bad for twenty years.

The programs always make me extraordinarily optimistic because I know that what we are doing works. What makes me pessimistic or disillusioned is the feeling you get sometimes that you are just beating your head against a wall. Change is very slow—not on the ground, but back here—I'm talking about the bigger picture, the political process, trying to convince people to care, to donate. These are the types of things that take a very long time. For example, there are times when we will be short-listed for a major grant or a major donation and yet in the end we may not get it, for reasons of policy or popularity or expediency—you name it. And the reality of those decisions is life and death. I hate having to make those phone calls, I hate having to say to our partners, "Look, we're going to have to scale it right back because no one wants to support AIDS orphans in Ethiopia right now and we've tried, we've exhausted every means possible, I've been on my hands and knees for eight months and everybody said no." That is what kills me. It is not the lack of change, it is seeing the opportunities that are wasted.

You have referred to a "paradoxical sadness and joy

that inevitably come with a 'calling.'"

There is that sort of excitement and peace of mind that comes from knowing you are trying to change things. I get up every day and I think about the people that we have lost to war and the people we are trying to help overseas and I can get through my day because I know we are trying to do something about it. That's the joy. The sadness comes from feeling like you are being pushed down, that you are being sidelined or marginalized, or passed over because of politics or disinterest or apathy. The reasons why people do not want to get involved are plentiful and, unfortunately, the reasons why they do are often very few. And it is intensely rewarding and intensely frustrating. Sometimes it's intensely rewarding and intensely frustrating all within the same hour.

And are the people around you at risk of burning out?

Oh gosh, yeah. You are always at risk of being burnt out. You sometimes feel like you just don't know where the energy is going to come from. I have wrestled with that myself. It's a real risk for people who work in our office and those who work on our field projects. It's tough. You have to know when to say, "I need some time," though sometimes the moments when you really need that time are the moments when you are least able to take it. This is the reason why, as an organization, we have very strict policies around overtime and vacation—we're trying to ensure that staff don't get to that point because the risk is very real. But for me, again, the only thing that does make me get up everyday, even when I am feeling like that, is that I know that I am lucky, I am lucky to be here, and I am lucky to have the opportunities to do what I am doing. I have adored people who no longer have those opportunities, who have died in the process of doing this work, so I also wrestle with the knowledge that it's self-indulgent to say, "Well, poor me, I can't face my day today." Seems pretty pathetic.

Do you consider yourself to be a pacifist?

I consider myself to be a peace activist. I think there is a difference between the two. I think that there are times when pacifism is the appropriate response. I also think there are times when you need to refuse to be pacified, to use everything at your disposal in terms of the voice that you have and maybe some of the public opportunities that you have to bear witness to human rights abuses that are taking place in other parts of the world. And that doesn't mean shutting up and taking it on the chin, it means being prepared to stand up and be a voice for what you believe is right and fair.

Are there thinkers or historical humanitarian actors you look to as an inspiration?

Absolutely, there are lots of them. Roméo Dallaire has been a very, very powerful voice urging us to critically examine how we protect and respond to the needs of civilians in other parts of the world. Stephen Lewis, Nelson Mandela, Graça Machel—who has done a lot of work on war-affected children globally. Lloyd Axworthy is someone I have a great deal of respect for. Dr. James Orbinski, who is a great guy, chairperson of our board, and the past President of Médecins Sans Frontières (Doctors Without Borders).

Ursula Franklin. And of course my husband, Dr. Eric Hoskins (President of War Child Canada). Actually, I look around me and I see a lot of people committed to change and who have been very active in raising the level of awareness and understanding of Canadians, as well as raising our level of support for global issues. I have a great deal of admiration for all of them.

What about Bernard Kouchner, one of the founders of Médecins Sans Frontères?

Over the course of his career he has generated considerable debate around humanitarian action. That kind of public discourse is always a positive thing.

But he's also made the jump into politics (currently he is France's minister of foreign affairs). What do you think about making the jump to politics?

I don't think I could stand to be that unpopular (laughs). It is not being a politician that is the obstacle, in my mind, it is the political process. I don't think I am ready for that at this stage in my life. My husband was Lloyd Axworthy's Senior Policy Advisor for four years when we were living in Ottawa so I saw what they went through. At this point, I am really happy to see the immediacy of our actions. We do a proposal, we raise some funds, we have a program, and it is making a difference. It's immediate. I do not know that I have the patience or the tenacity to be one step removed from that change at this point in my life. But maybe this will evolve, you never know.

2

Canada at War

As Canadians, we tend to think of ourselves as a peace-keeping nation and I think many of us assume that when it comes to war and peace our government is on the right side and there is no need to fret. You do not see things that way.

I do not see things that way. We are more than 40th in the world in terms of our contribution to peace-keeping globally. We are at .29% of our GNI (Gross National Income) in terms of our contribution to ODA (Overseas Development Assistance) annually—14th in the world. The UN target of 0.7% was set by Lester B. Pearson in 1969. Thirty-eight years later we are still not standing by the very principles that we laid out. So we rely a lot on our history as it was taught to us, but it is history, it is not a reality. If we want to have that role in the world again, if we want to be seen as the honest brokers, if we want to be seen as the middle moral power, if we want a place at the table brokering peace agreements and being seen as a reliable, trustworthy partner, then we need to—and there is no other way around it—we need to step up and be more Canadian. Because particularly in the last seven years we have been less Canadian, I believe, than at any time in our history.

I read your dispatch from Afghanistan for Maclean's

magazine a few years ago. Are Canadians getting enough of these stories—thorny, human stories that are told without an overweening patriotic undertone? Why is it important for Canadians to know these stories?

You absolutely need to get the human story. I say this all the time: War is not about who wins and who loses, but about who lives and who dies. Whether you're talking about soldiers, whether you're talking about civilians, whether you're talking about peacekeepers, it is the human side of the war that is, in my mind, the most important story to be told. And unfortunately, that is often the story that gets sidelined in favour of stories presenting bigger, strategic kinds of analyses. Now we need some of this, but we also need to humanize war, or at least the impact of war, so we can fully appreciate the cost of it. Only then will Canadians be able to make legitimate and informed decisions about whether or not it is worth that price.

I do think there are some amazing Canadian reporters who have done remarkable things, Stephanie Nolan, Brian Stewart, Tom Kennedy, Mark McKinnon Stephen Puddicombe— we've crossed paths with many of these journalists overseas, even shared dodgy flights, bad scotch, and war stories with more than a few of them. They are extraordinarily courageous and they represent a legacy of honesty and compassion in Canadian journalism. I should also mention Paul Watson who wrote the book Where War Lives, which was an extremely powerful and provocative book. I applaud their efforts. The difficulty is, we are such a pop culture-obsessed society, and increasingly so. I remember that the same week Kenya was imploding, Britney Spears was going back into a psychiatric hospital and that was what was on Larry King. My husband and I sat there together dumbfounded, asking ourselves how it could be possible that there is so little opportunity for real news.

And the excuse from media networks is always the same—and I am touching on this very superficially— that, well, "We give the viewers what they want and this is what brings in the ratings." But sometimes you also have to give them what they need to know, not just what's titillating. That is the responsibility that you have as a broadcaster. But as the media has become more and more consolidated, there is less room for those divergent points of view and for those interesting reflections and commentary. I find that to be very disappointing, at least for the mainstream media. Now a lot of plugged-in people are engaging alternative forms of media but you really have to seek it out and that makes our job, as an organization that much harder. It means that you when you get in front of an audience and start talking about Africa, there's very little awareness. You find yourself having to go further and further back just to impart a very baseline level of understanding of the areas and the issues that you're trying to tackle. If people have no concept at all of the countries in which you are working or the issues you are tackling it is that much harder to convince them to support your efforts.

Right now there is a debate about how long Canadian soldiers should be in Kandahar. Do you feel this debate is anchored enough in the human reality of the war in Afghanistan right now?

In the midst of all this discussion about whether we should be there and when we should leave, we are not asking some of the more critical questions about what Canada's development priorities should even be in Afghanistan. If the objective is to bring peace and security to Afghanistan, then that is what we need to be focusing on, that is why we need to be looking more systematically at our role in promoting development, because this is a war that will not end unless there are real humanitarian and development solutions that are consistently applied.

For example, as Canadians we need to be asking question such as, how can we best support their transition toward democracy? What does that actually look like? How do we strengthen civil society? How do we put an end to corruption? How do we strengthen their judiciary and put an end to the culture of impunity? These are the kinds of questions that I think Canadians have expertise in and that we need to be asking more specifically. Those are the issues that are not being debated enough and I see a lot of opportunities that are being missed as a result.

I am also concerned about the amount of criticism I have heard, claiming NGO humanitarian actors are in the way in Afghanistan, that the military is best equipped to handle Afghanistan's reconstruction. You have to be very careful if you are participating in a conflict to clearly delineate between what is peace and security and what is reconstruction and development. If you are rebuilding a hospital and it is seen as just an extension of the military apparatus, the level of receptivity and acceptability of that effort, no matter how noble we may think it is, will not be high. NGOs (both local and international) must have a significant role moving forward because they are best equipped, and have the most experience, when it comes to working with local communities, facilitating the transition towards peace and reconciliation, ensuring community buy-in and building—in a meaningful and participatory way—local capacity and local ownership. This is critical in facilitating the transition towards a peaceful solution in Afghanistan, and this is why our ODA policies matter.

Have you found people who work in the Canadian Armed Forces receptive to your message in general?

In my experience, people serving in the Canadian military overseas are receptive to many aspects of the message. They want to see peace and stability, they want to see reconstruction go ahead, they understand what human rights mean, and many of them are there because they believe they are promoting and protecting human security. Too many of them have paid with their lives in defence of these goals. Where we tend to draw the line, for example, is on issues such as whether we should ban cluster munitions, reduce our military exports, or impose limits on the transference of small arms—that's where our views often diverge.

When you look at a situation like the Congo or Sudan, in the context of what's happened in Iraq and Afghanistan, are you reluctant to call for a government like ours to get involved?

There are two ways that government can get involved. One is through our ODA and another is by responding to a call for peacekeepers in situations where that call has been made. Congo currently has 16,000 UN peacekeepers and there are Canadians advising the peacekeeping forces, but there's still room for us to do more. Canada has not, up until now, committed peace-keepers to Sudan. There is always a role for Canada to play in these contexts but it requires human and financial capital. I believe we have the human capital. I am always astounded by the number of people who are really interested and really engaged in this kind of work. What we need is more financial capital. That's why our ODA is so important—it allows us to have a more substantive role on an international level. The kind of role that is often identified with Canada but that we've fallen short of in recent years.

3

Getting people's attention

Do you ever get a backlash from people who support these wars, people who think you have an agenda or that your politics are counter to theirs, or not patriotic enough?

When you run an NGO, people are going to criticize you for all kinds of reasons. For example, if we talk about the exploitation of resources in a war-torn country and some of the reprehensible behaviour of some multinationals operating within those countries, people will stand up and say, "We need to have investment in Africa in order to have development, and they're entitled to this and people like you are part of the problem." And that's fair enough, they are allowed to have opinions. My message is always one of responsibility; it's not a question of whether they should be investing in Africa but a question of how they are investing—is it fair, ethical and transparent? Those are the bigger questions that I want to see asked and answered appropriately.

You must also have people who say, "Those are nice ideas Sam, and the world needs idealists, but we have to be realistic." How do you respond?

I would say that, first of all, I do not consider myself to be an idealist, I consider myself to be a realist. I look at what we can do in the context of what can be achieved. And so I do not for a second believe that we will be in a situation where there will not be war in the world. And I do not for a second believe that all conflicts are unavoidable, and I do believe that sometimes you do have to use military force to prosecute those who are attacking civilians and who need to be stopped. I don't shy away from that debate. I'm not a woman with a shortage of opinions (laughs).

At the same time, I think that it is very easy to dismiss people who believe in the value of peace as being somehow naive or idealistic or poorly informed. That is the kind of rhetoric that you hear all the time. Coincidentally, in my experience that rhetoric often tends to come from people who have spent very little, if any, time working in war zones, very little time liaising with those on the ground, very little time investing in understanding the local culture and the local context and in working to develop locally driven solutions to the problems those communities are facing. So that kind of criticism I find to be quite flippant, often baseless, but at the same time—let's have a discussion. Let's look at the facts and then let's make a decision around who's being realistic and who's being naive and who's being rhetorical and who's being aggressive and who really isn't looking at the entire elephant. Every time I do get into those discussions, it forces me to think through my own arguments more critically and that's a good thing.

You have spent a lot of time in the Congo and that seems like a good example of an enormous conflict— perhaps more people have died in that war than in any other since the Second World War—that no one talks about much here. But it is still very far away. Why should young Canadians feel more connected to that conflict?

I think young Canadians should feel connected to any conflict that is happening around the world. Sometimes we are connected to those conflicts directly, but if we care about human rights, if we care about social justice, then the inhumanity of war anywhere threatens everything we hold most dear as people. So we need to feel connected to it simply on a human level. But also, war in the Congo is primarily about resources, and has been for almost 200 years. It started with the Belgians with the rubber trade. It has also been about corruption, the instability that was created during the Rwandan genocide, various ethnic divisions, and on and on. But at the heart of the war in the Congo has been a struggle financed by and driven by the need to control resources and the wealth that comes from those resources. That includes diamonds and other precious stones, metals and minerals, and timber.

And there is a mineral in the Congo called coltan (tantalum), which is a conducting element. And it is found in almost all of our cell-phones, in our video game consoles, and in our computers. The Congo is believed to contain the world's largest coltan deposits. In fact a couple of years ago the UN convened a panel of experts to study this issue. They cited 114 companies and 54 individuals who were in violation of OECD (Organization for Economic Co-operation and Development) guidelines for multinational enterprises in connection with the war in the Congo. That's things like companies benefiting from the direct assistance of combatants and companies participating in military action. Some of those were Canadian companies. So when we think, "Oh, there's war happening in another part of the world that has nothing to do with us," we don't have to go very far to see that connection. All we have to do is answer an email or pick up our cell-phone and that connection is very much alive.

Do young people respond to that message?

I hope so. I think that when you're trying to connect people to these issues, you have to make those connections real on an intellectual level and you have to make those connections real on an emotional level to see that these are innately human stories.

What's interesting to me about a lot of young people now, people between the ages of fifteen and thirty, is that they have grown up in a very international context. From the time they were little, they were hearing about Somalia, Rwanda, the former Yugoslavia, Iraq, Afghanistan—these have been present for them. On top of that they know we are facing environmental degradation and climate change and what that means. So they understand that actions and inactions have consequences. And the way that you engage them is quite different from the way you engage people who are worried about their mortgage and getting their kids to soccer practice. Because younger people, their reality has always been a global reality—they're plugged in, they're turned on, they're paying attention. Not all of them, but a larger proportion of them than people of the baby boomer generation. In this current global climate we can no longer afford to be self-interested.

4

War Child Canada's activities and message

Is there a particular project of War Child's right now that you especially like to talk about, a project that you feel really represents the work of the organization?

There are lots of them. We have a big program in Darfur right now where we are serving about 100,000 internally displaced people. We are focusing on providing safe spaces for kids and on child protection, and livelihood training for young people to prevent them from being recruited into the armed militias. We are teaching youth bricklaying and other very tangible skills so they are able to earn an income for themselves and for their families. We are also working with young girls and women on more gender-specific activities. So the project is doing two things: providing psychological support and poverty relief for those families that are trapped in very difficult circumstances, and it is also preventing the inevitability of increasing numbers of young people being caught up in the conflict. It is an interesting humanitarian program that has an emergency dimension to it as well as a prevention dimension, and that is why, for us anyhow, it is something I am particularly proud of.

We also have an amazing access to justice program in northern Uganda. We have Canadian lawyers training local lawyers and local legal aid groups to represent children, defend their rights, do community training to end gender-based violence, and strengthen the rights of children in the north. We are also training the police and the judiciary. The program is about ending a culture of impunity, where it is okay to beat or injure or abuse a child and get away with it. That particular project is ground breaking and we are looking to expand it to Sudan and a couple of other locations this year, and all of us at War Child Canada are very excited by that.

As an organization, we are always trying to reinvent the model, to push the envelope and to see how we can break the cycle of violence and poverty and despair plaguing many war torn nations. Now that we are in our eighth year of programming, I am seeing many countries in which we have been operating, where that is actually happening and it is very, very encouraging.

On the subject of your local partners, is it harder to find them or to sustain them once you find them?

You always have extraordinarily talented people on the ground. Sometimes those people are not well organized, they have a lot of really good ideas and they are really connected at the community level, but what they need is to be empowered, they need their capacity built, and there are many ways you can do that. So it is not difficult to identify them. What tends to be difficult is to create enough momentum around your work that people will actively support it. One problem is that you are often dealing with areas that people have mostly forgotten, whether you are talking about the Congo or Sierra Leone or Sri Lanka, people have moved on. They are focusing on Iraq, they are focusing on Afghanistan, so it can be really hard to mobilize support back home for those efforts. But you cannot have a project unless you have funding—that's the reality.

The trick for any organization is to not be so hand-to-mouth and the easiest way to achieve that is to grow your financial base, particularly through people who are monthly donors. Then you know that they are invested in the organization and you can rely on them, and it means your partners can rely on you because you know where the revenue is coming from to fund your programs. It is dependable—not subject to the whims and mercies of what is happening globally and where the media may or may not be.

Less than 5% of Canadian donations each year go to support international charities. War Child Canada has an annual budget of between 3.5 and 4 million dollars—that includes about half a million dollars in in-kind donations each year. Ninety cents on every dollar goes to our overseas programming. Overall, we are a small organization competing for a very small piece of a very small pie. And it's tough, it's very tough. Fundraising is the hardest part of my job.

I have read you discussing the importance of empathy to your work. How hard is to generate empathy for people suffering in other countries, and especially trying to get away from the clichés?

We have certain standards that we adhere to very strictly. We do not use any images of children that we consider demeaning or exploitative, like pictures of kids in extreme poverty. My feeling is that those tend to play into a lot of the misconceptions we have in Canada about those living with war and poverty, and yet there is great strength and great resilience and great spirit and tremendous capacity, for example, in Africa. That is what we need to be emphasizing and encouraging Canadians to support.

We also need to be responding from a place of information as opposed to a place of guilt. So when War Child Canada puts its message out there we try to focus on a positive, constructive, or even at times thought-provoking message. We want people to respond because they're passionate, because they believe something isn't right, and because they want to do something about it. Not because they just think, "Oh, if I send my ten dollars to War Child Canada I won't have to feel guilty every time one of those images pops up."

Is it a strange space to be in, the NGO space, where there are activists you cannot quite join with, but then you are not on the other side either? Is it hard to get used to?

It is hard to get used to. As a charity you have to be cautious and that means you are not always a free agent. There are real and important limits, for example, to a charity's participation in anything that would be considered " political". There are times when that can feel very constraining. But then War Child Canada is also part of a number of NGO coalitions: the coalition to stop the use of child soldiers, the coalition to end the use of cluster munitions, and many others that have constructive, engaging messages. And, of course, we would not be able to do the work that we're doing if we weren't a charity. So you gain in some areas what you lose in others, but you must always be cognizant of these restrictions.

Although for me, the whole concept of charity is a loaded proposition. I mean, it's called 'charity', but for me it is not about that. For me it is about our common humanity and what we stand for. When you say charity, you make it sound as if it is optional. As if it's optional for us to be globally aware, to be socially responsible citizens. It is not optional. In the same way you do not drive down the 401 anymore and roll down the window and throw the garbage out, as many people used to do in the seventies, we need to make it socially unacceptable that we allow exploitation and abuse to happen in other parts of the world in our name and for our convenience.

Tell me about the role music has played in your activism. What got you thinking about music as the best way to reach young people?

Music has always had a very strong affiliation with the anti-war movement. So for us it was very logical. With art and activism there is such a close association, it makes intuitive sense. We also, very early on, connected with Denise Donlon, who was running MuchMusic at that time. For us, that was really key, when the relationship to music really cemented. And it has grown from there. We've worked with many outstanding Canadian and international artists, including Radiohead, The Tragically Hip, Our Lady Peace, Chantal Kreviazuk, Sum 41, Sarah McLachlan, David Usher, K-Os, Avril Lavigne. They've lent their time, their talent and their celebrity to the cause, and we don't ever take that for granted. The challenge is that there can be a perception, that because you've worked with some high profile artists, that as an organization you are drowning in donations. This isn't true. In our case, the music is often a way to generate attention and interest but doesn't necessarily result in increased revenues. At the same time, it is because of this music-driven awareness over the years that we've been able to make people aware of the organization, and it is the reason why, since our inception, we have never paid for advertising.

You were talking before about how our society has become very pop culture-fed, do you feel like there's a tension—

Do I feel like I'm talking out of both sides of my mouth—or other body parts—you mean? (Laughs). Exploiting pop culture on the one hand, and criticizing it on the other? I think you have to be careful around how you use celebrity or pop culture to get your message out. It has to be the right kind of celebrity, the right kind of opportunity, and it has to be dignified. I can't define what I mean by dignified but when it's undignified I know what it looks like. I do think you need to go to where people are in as many ways as possible. Some people will go to a university lecture, others will not. Some people will pick up a CD, others will not. At the same time, I would never ever advocate doing one at the expense of the other. You cannot have something exclusively on Entertainment Tonight and never on the CBC. Doesn't make any sense. You have to have the meat...and the potatoes.

Which is which?

(Laughing) I don't know, it depends on how many donations we get, that's how we measure it.

Do you do more outreach with young people than any other demographic?

We do a lot with youth and teachers. I get a lot of energy from them. I believe we are going to see more and more people concerned and committed and engaged in international issues and thinking in a more globally responsible fashion. And that is very encouraging to me.

Teachers know they are shaping the minds of the future, that the next generation of intellectuals, creators, investment bankers, and politicians is sitting in their classrooms, and they feel the weight of that responsibility. My experience of teachers is they take that very seriously, they feel it is an important part of their legacy. If we can help them achieve that through the educational resources we develop—for example, study guides and lesson plans on various global issues—that War Child Canada creates, then that is a really important way to get your message out. We conducted a survey a couple years ago with the polling firm Environics where we asked young people between 15 and 24 a number of questions on global issues, including: "What's the single most important source of information to you when it comes to global issues?" They had a bunch of choices, including the internet, media, friends and family, et cetera. And 75% of them said teachers—their single most important source of information. This is why we work so closely with schools and teachers to bring these issues into the classroom—education is the very foundation of social change. But you have to start early to spark that curiosity and interest.

You have talked about the idea of socially responsible, global citizenship. When you think about what it means to be a globally aware citizen, how do you define that?

People thinking in global terms. When they choose which companies to invest in or to support, when they ask questions about how they live their life—Are they going to buy a conflict diamond or not buy a conflict diamond? Are they going to invest in cluster munitions or are they are not going to invest in cluster munitions? Do they support privatized water? All of these are global questions. For me, a global citizen is somebody who asks those questions even if he or she does not know the answers. It is the fact of asking them, of trying to wrestle and think about these critically, that counts. And that is the first step toward being globally responsible.

Do you see this happening?

I see it happening more. I also see a lot of excuses. I see a lot of pension fund managers saying, "We can't eliminate the top ten arms manufacturers from the portfolio because we'll never make any money." But at some point we have to be prepared to sacrifice. We have to be prepared to say that financial returns don't trump ethics. And instead of having a 10% return, maybe I'm okay with a 9% return. And it is worth that price. We are going in that direction increasingly in the environmental context and I'd like to see us doing that in the context of war as well—for example, changing the way that we export our arms so we consider a country's human rights record more critically.

Okay, but is this something a 15-year-old in Manitoba can do, is there something for those people as well?

Absolutely. They are not the ones out there buying diamond engagement rings and they are not the ones out there investing in cluster munitions manufacturers. At the same time, they might be buying products from companies that are implicated in conflicts around the world. Coltan very much affects them. These are important questions for them too.

Moreover, they are eventually going to inherit this legacy of war, or whatever it looks like in ten, twenty years. And so it's incumbent upon them to be investing in humanitarian and development solutions to war, now—not tomorrow, not the next day, not ten years from now, but now. And it does not have to be a lot. Even if they decide, "You know what, I'm not going to wait for my government to commit 0.7% to ODA, I'm going to commit .0.7% of my income," for every hundred dollars they bring in, that's seventy cents. The statement it makes is profound and important. Each year thousands of young people participate in Gulu Walk—of which War Child Canada is one of the beneficiaries—and this year, for the second year running, students will walk for eight days in Alberta to raise funds for Darfur as part of the Walk for Darfur campaign. The idea, which is wholly theirs, is to walk 300,000 paces for each of the 300,000 people who have lost their lives as a result of the tragedy unfolding in that region. It's very inspiring. These are just a few of the ways that students can do something, though this list is by no means exhaustive.

When people ask you, What is the most important thing that we can be doing globally, how do you answer?

Increasingly I have become convinced that a huge part of our emphasis needs to be on girls' education. When you look at one of the single most important demographic determinants of whether a child lives to his or her fifth birthday, it all comes down to a woman's access to economic power, which is by extension an educational indicator. That to me is such a critical piece. When you look at unstable parts of the world, and you meet these kids, the single most important thing they ask you for is the opportunity to go to school. And the more we can invest, particularly in young girls, to give them tools to help them become literate, to empower them, that is one of the single most effective and important contributions that Canadians can make, in terms of promoting peace and security and stability globally.

It's funny, I'm a public health doctor. When I started this business, I was all about vaccinating kids, I thought it was the most important thing we could do. And here I am fourteen years later saying actually, a critical priority is education. We have to get girls into school and provide those opportunities for them. Because that's going to promote peace and stability and that's going to help bring about an end to the AIDS crisis, and that's going to mean a substantial decrease in child mortality. It doesn't mean we do not do other things as well. But in terms of bang for our buck, that to me is the biggest one. It's the reason why, in recent years, War Child Canada has oriented a considerable amount of its programming towards women and girls' education—rebuilding schools, training teachers, and working with communities to promote girls' access to education and improve female literacy rates. We've made this a priority in the Congo, Afghanistan, Iraq, Ethiopia, Sudan, and in many other of our target countries.

Will you have the same job in five years?

For me, this job has changed so much since I started in 1999 and that is what has kept it really interesting. I have gone from being the person who participated in almost all the hands-on work overseas, as well as all the evaluations, and the assessments, and report-writing, and proposal development, to where I am now, where I spend a lot more time with fundraising and public engagement, and with public speaking and writing, not to mention human resources, management, and leading the team here together with my husband and War Child Canada President Dr. Eric Hoskins. I'm always changing and always evolving and trying to do what I think will work best.

I also think you can hang on too long. I think when you start an organization you can impede its growth if you do not make room for other people to leave their mark and to have ownership of it. I do not know when that moment is going to come for me, but I know I am surrounded by people who will tell me.

You're not going to wait as long as Fidel Castro?

No (laughs). I'm committed to this charity and even if

the nature of my work here may change and the nature of my role may change, I will always believe in it.

This interview reflects Dr. Samantha Nutt's personal views and experiences and not necessarily those of War Child Canada.

About the Authors

Dr. Samantha Nutt is the Founder and Executive Director of War Child Canada. Over the past fourteen years, Dr. Nutt has worked in some of the world's most violent flash points with War Child Canada, the United Nations and non-governmental organizations (NGOs), including Iraq, Afghanistan, The Democratic Republic of Congo, Liberia, Sierra Leone, Somalia, Iraq, Burundi, northern Uganda, and the Thai-Burmese border.

A specialist in Maternal and Child Health in zones of armed conflict, Family Medicine, Public Health, and Women's Health, Nutt is also on staff at Sunnybrook and Women's Health Science Centre and is an Assistant Professor at the University of Toronto in the Department of Family and Community Medicine. Nutt holds undergraduate degrees in Arts and Science, and in Medicine, from McMaster University, and postgraduate degrees in Medicine and in Public Health from the University of Toronto as well as the London School of Hygiene and Tropical Medicine (London University). She recently received Honorary Doctorates from McMaster University, Brock University, and Niagara University for her work promoting human rights and her role in delivering humanitarian assistance to some of the world's most vulnerable populations.

Chosen by *Maclean's* magazine for their annual Honour Roll as one of "12 Canadians Making a Difference", Dr. Samantha Nutt is a role model to many Canadians and has received numerous humanitarian awards for her work in support of war-affected children, including the 2007 Tiffany Mark Award. Nutt is the recipient of "Canada's Top 40 Under 40 Award" (as featured in *The Globe and Mail*), has been profiled by *TIME Magazine* as "One of Canada's Five Leading Activists," and celebrated on CTV National News as a Canadian "Success Story," among many other honours.

War Child Canada is a registered charity dedicated to providing urgently needed humanitarian assistance and sustainable development support to war-affected children around the world. The organization is currently implementing programs in ten war-torn regions around the world and also generates awareness, support, and action for children's rights everywhere. In addition, War Child Canada has domestic outreach programs in schools and among youth across Canada and the United States. For more information please visit www.warchild.ca.

Daniel Aldana Cohen is a Toronto-based writer and editor. He has covered Canadian and South American politics and social movements for a number of newspapers and magazines in Canada and abroad, including *The Toronto Star*, *The Walrus* and *The New Internationalist*. He is a co-editor of *Notes from Canada's Young Activists: A Generation Stands up for Change* (for which Nutt wrote the "Foreward") and a contributor to *GreenTOpia: Toward a Sustainable Toronto*.